Separated and Waiting—God's Way

Survival Tips for the Person
Trying to Save Their Marriage Alone

THE INTERNATIONAL CENTER
FOR RECONCILING GOD'S WAY

ISBN: 978-1-952369-04-9

LCCN: 2020917205

Published by EA Books Publishing,
a division of Living Parables of Central Florida, Inc. a 501c3

*A special thank you to all who shared
their stories and to the ministry partners
who shared their insight and expertise.*

WELCOME MESSAGE FROM

the International Center for Reconciling God's Way

www.icrgw.org

The International Center for Reconciling God's Way (ICRGW) is a faith-based, non-profit organization that provides help and hope for marriages in crisis. While the focus of this ministry is to see all couples reconcile, there are times when a physical separation occurs which sometimes ends in divorce. *Separated and Waiting God's Way*, is a nine-week resource for people who are separated. The founders of the ICRGW, Joe and Michelle Williams, are the authors of *Yes, Your Marriage Can Be Saved*, (Focus on the Family, 2007), and co-authors of the *Marriage 911: First Response* twelve-week workbook (in partnership with The National Institute of Marriage). Because they experienced a two-year separation in their own marriage, they understand what it takes to reconcile. They, along with the other leaders in the organization, have provided support for hundreds of couples in crisis and reconciliation resources for church leaders over the years. Collectively, they share their expertise in this resource.

If you are reading this welcome message, you are more than likely in the midst of or facing a physical separation. It is our goal, over the next nine weeks, to provide the tools that you will need to foster a climate of reconciliation in your marriage. By doing so, you will avoid making hasty decisions that often result in pushing your spouse even further away. We call this "holding the line of reconciliation." The word "we" will always refer to statements used by all of us in the organization unless otherwise noted.

As you go through the weekly lessons, it is recommended that you have a Bible and a journal to record your progress and what the Lord shows you in the Scripture readings. The Scriptures are from the *New Living Testament Study Bible*, unless otherwise noted. It is good to read all passages surrounding the Bible verses when applying them to your situation. While traditions and cultures change over time, God's principles are true to any generation or culture. This resource can be used prior or as a follow-up to the *Marriage 911: First Response* twelve-week workbook. It is helpful if you read *Yes, Your Marriage Can Be Saved* for more tools. All resources are available through our website.

Please do your best to trust God as you do the lessons. Allow Him to provide peace and strength during what can oftentimes be an emotionally painful journey. Over the years, we have seen husbands and wives reconcile even in the most hopeless situations. We have also shared in the pain and disappointment with those whose marriages ended in divorce. You will read some of their stories. While their names and a few details have been changed to protect their identity, their stories and situations are true. One common thread when working with separated couples is that often a person who walks away from his or her spouse will feel an unexplainable pull back to the marriage. Chances are your spouse will want to reconcile before you have even finished the lessons. That would be wonderful. But, if not, consider this a time when you and God will grow closer as He shows you things you would otherwise never have known. It is also possible that you are the one who originally wanted to separate but are now having second thoughts. If that is the case, please complete the weekly lessons and give your marriage a chance.

The cares of this world tend to take us away from quiet times with the Lord, while suffering tends to draw us to Him. The ICRGW leadership team is praying for you and believes that God can and will do a supernatural work in your marriage, as you focus on Him through this study.

CONTENTS

FOREWORD   vii

BEFORE YOU BEGIN   ix

LESSON ONE: LONELINESS

     How to be proactive in times of loneliness.

LESSON TWO: FINANCIAL STRAIN   8

     How to get creative when facing challenges affecting your financial security.

LESSON THREE: BETRAYAL   14

     How to stay emotionally and spiritually healthy when a promise is broken.

LESSON FOUR: LACK OF PURPOSE   19

     How to press on when your reason to exist comes into question.

LESSON FIVE: VULNERABILITY   28

     How to avoid giving in to temptation.

LESSON SIX: ALIENATION   35

     How to face feelings of isolation.

LESSON SEVEN: UNHEALTHY FEAR   42

     How to be proactive against unhealthy fear (False Evidence Appearing Real).

LESSON EIGHT: EMOTIONAL INSTABILITY   48

     How to get back up when circumstances beyond your control get you down.

LESSON NINE: LOSS OF IDENTITY   53

     How to identify your essential character God's way.

CONCLUDING REMARKS   59

GROUP DISCUSSION AND FACILIATOR GUIDELINES   60

FOREWORD

From Mary Lynn

I actually started thinking about divorce a couple of weeks into my marriage. I felt I was in over my head. The thought of divorce was my way out and a safety net. Even though I was a Christian, my walk with God was based more on wanting to be happy rather than holy. A couple of years into our marriage, in the midst of bickering one day, I told my husband to leave, and he did. I did not want him back, but each time I tried to seek a legal separation through an attorney, I kept hearing this small still voice saying, "Don't do this, don't do this." It made no sense to me. I was not employed, and it was scary to have to trust that my husband would provide for me without him being legally required to do so. In the midst of my turmoil, I began to turn my focus to the Lord and His Word. I was attending church, but most people did not know what was really going on behind the scenes at home. I had no support system. I felt alone. A couple of months later, the Lord began to reveal to me how I had contributed to the downfall of our marriage. I knew I would have to go to my husband and ask forgiveness. When I met with my husband and asked his forgiveness, he said he forgave me but was not coming back home. I was devastated.

I tried everything to get him to reconsider, but my desperate attempts just pushed him further away. While searching the Internet one day, looking for help, I came across the International Center for Reconciling God's Way and the Marriage 911 resources. I attended a twelve-week course for women only that was being offered in my community, and found the support I needed. Through the lessons, I began to understand the importance of changing my focus from trying to win my husband back to focusing on becoming a spiritually and emotionally healthy person. The course leader explained that by spending my energy and time on becoming a godly woman and learning to trust God in all circumstances, I would be ready to reconcile if and when my spouse might have a change of heart. "This stance", she said, "is what we in this ministry refer to as the line of reconciliation." Each time I began to worry about finances or being alone, and considered taking things into my own hands through an attorney, I would hear her words: "Stay on the line of reconciliation."

I am so grateful that I did not seek an attorney or file for a legal separation or divorce, even though nearly everyone I went to for help told me to do so—including a few church leaders. Financially, doors opened in amazing ways, and I have learned to trust God's promises to provide for my needs. One of the ministry leaders in the reconciliation class said, "It is not our money anyway, it is the Lord's." While it seemed crazy not to seek legal protection, I knew that God was asking me to "not lean on my own understanding," as it says in Proverbs.

The most important lesson I have learned through this separation is that God is not a liar. He will provide. It may be at the last minute and in a way I never expected, but He will do it. Will my spouse decide to return home? I don't know, but I do know that I will remain on the "line of reconciliation" and continue to trust God to work behind the scenes. Regardless of how this ends, I am now prepared to face my future with a supernatural strength and joy that only God could have given me.

Separated and waiting—God's way

BEFORE YOU BEGIN

It is best to go through these lessons in a small, same-gender group in order to have the support and accountability you will need. Each person should have their own book. Video teachings and testimonies are available on the website, and the facilitator guidelines are at the back of this book. Let your spouse know that you are going through this resource, and ask him or her to consider doing the same. Sometimes a spouse who has been unwilling to work on reconciliation just needs a nudge to see hope. Regardless of your spouse's response, for the next nine weeks, do not file for a separation or divorce. Let God work. If you are already in the midst of a legal process that can't be stopped, just continue to do your part in creating an atmosphere of reconciliation. We have witnessed miracles when just one spouse does his or her part to save their marriage. We have also known couples who have remarried after a divorce is final. Until one person dies or remarries, it is never too late.

If you are unable to be in a group, consider asking someone of the same gender to go through the book with you. Having a support system in place is vital when a marriage is in crisis. While the weekly lessons can provide wisdom and direction, there is nothing like person-to-person support. God often uses others to be "Jesus with skin on," as many have said. Do your best to create the support you need.

As mentioned, you will need a Bible to look up Scriptures and a journal to record your thoughts as you go through the weekly lessons. Do your best not to get discouraged. Your marriage crisis did not happen overnight and neither will your reconciliation. We know from experience that when one spouse makes a behavior change, the other spouse will usually have trouble adjusting. Even good change often causes an upheaval in relationships. Each person has a role that has become habit. So, don't give up if your spouse responds to your healthy changes in a negative way. Just keep your focus on doing what's right and becoming a person who will survive your marital crisis in a way that honors God. If you have children, remember that they are watching. The saying many of us have heard never rings truer than when facing marriage problems: "When parenting, do your best, and use words when necessary."

Please feel free to contact us for prayer as you go through the lessons. When you have completed the nine weeks, we can help with whatever follow-up you may need. Our ministry team is available through the website and all prayer requests are prayed for. All questions are answered within 24 hours by real people, and your email will not be shared with any other organization.

We are praying for you.

LONELINESS

The Lord is close to all who call on Him, yes, to all who call on him in truth.

—

Psalm 145:18

We all feel lonely at times. Even married couples living under the same roof can feel alone if their spouse is not meeting some of their emotional or sexual needs. If your spouse is no longer residing in the home, you more than likely have experienced feelings of loneliness that go beyond the norm. When a married couple physically separates, there is an emotional and spiritual tearing apart of the heart. We have heard abandoned spouses say that it is like their mate died—but worse. One reason they feel this way is that, unlike being widowed, they know their spouse made a choice to leave.

Feelings of loneliness occur when you least expect them. This is true even for the spouse who initiated the separation. A common antidote for feeling lonely is to get emotionally or sexually involved with someone other than your spouse. Be prepared. Don't fall prey to temptation and end up creating consequences that will result in even more emotional pain.

Some of the people who we have provided help for over the years, shared their experience of dealing with loneliness while they were separated.

From Phil

> *My first response when my wife moved out was to panic. I begged her to reconsider and come back. She did not want to talk to me, so I started writing her. She found this infuriating. I thought the loneliness would kill me. One minute I would be in absolute pieces, in pain like never before. Yet, the next minute I would sense God's presence and not feel so alone. As a result of this unexplainable peace, I began to pray more. I got a Bible and started reading a book on marriage that I found in the Christian section of a bookstore. Once I started changing my focus from my wife to God, my life changed. I still felt sad much of the time, but I felt that God was directing me and helping me stabilize my emotions. I continued to read books and the Bible, and met with counselors and a pastor. I continued to hold on to hope. When my*

wife and I talk, I am more relaxed, and she has commented on that. I am continuing to trust the outcome of my marriage to God.

From Tammy

When my husband left, I don't know that I specifically tried to win him back. To be honest, I was relieved because we had started arguing all the time. Our children were upset that he wasn't home, but the older ones even commented on the fact that it was more peaceful. However, once the dust settled, and it was evident that he wasn't coming home anytime soon, the loneliness set in. I found myself wanting him to come over just so I wouldn't be lonely, but not necessarily to talk about our marriage situation. This frustrated him, but I did not want to rehash things that had no immediate answers. When he gave me an ultimatum to either go for marriage counseling or he would stop coming over, I told him not to bother coming by anymore. Before long, though, the loneliness crept in. My children were not enough to fill the void that was missing having another adult in the home—even one that drove me crazy half the time.

Then, one day, while scrolling around on a social media site, I found myself typing the name of my first boyfriend in the search bar. It did not take long to reconnect with him and to feel that void filling. The problem was, that I found myself torn between doing what I knew in my heart was right and giving in to what felt so good. I only told a few trusted people about my situation. Even though I am a Christian, and the few that I told were also Christians, the advice I received was all over the place. The loneliness is nothing compared to the mess I created by getting someone else involved. I have since broken off the relationship, but I am not sure if my marriage will be saved.

From Joe

Michelle and I were separated three times, before we finally reconciled for good. The area of loneliness caused us both to make mistakes during the first two separations that nearly caused our marriage to end in divorce. One thing we often hear from someone who is trying to save their marriage alone, is that they feel unloved and unwanted. We understand how that feels, but to give in to those feelings is not the solution. The solution is getting a support system in place and turning your focus from your crisis to Christ. In our third separation—which lasted two years—we separately changed our focus and learned the tools that eventually led to our reconciliation.

From Michelle

When Joe and I were separated the third time, we were both attending church, but still focused on our problems instead of God. When I felt lonely, I would often go to Joe's apartment to be with him. I knew that we were still married in God's eyes, so I did not feel that I was doing anything wrong. However, by spending the night with him and going to my own place the next morning, I was sending mixed messages to Joe. It wasn't until he refused to let me spend the night, unless I was willing to work on our marriage, that I was forced to deal with the loneliness. As stated in our book, Yes, Your Marriage Can Be Saved, it was the loneliness that caused my focus to change to Christ. Being lonely is not always a bad thing. Some of the reconciliation tools that we learned, and now teach others, came as a result of our being lonely. We know now that God was using our painful separation to get our attention, and to reconcile with Him first. Your separation will not be easy, but it can be a time of spiritual and emotional growth while you wait.

Waiting, God's way, means you are being productive with your life and trusting that God is working, even if you can't feel it. This lesson will give you tips and Scripture passages to equip you in the area of loneliness.

Common Times of Loneliness

1. Mealtimes

Mealtimes often create an atmosphere of togetherness, even for couples in crisis. When separation occurs and one spouse is no longer sitting at the breakfast or dinner table, the empty chair brings an unwelcomed reminder of aloneness.

It is especially difficult for men and women who enjoy cooking, because there is suddenly one less person for whom to prepare a meal. For those who don't like to cook, it means trying to decide what and where to eat. Eating at restaurants once enjoyed as a couple can also trigger aloneness.

Proactive Tips

- Invite at least one family member or friend to dinner three or more times a week. This will help provide needed support and create an atmosphere for making sure you are eating healthier.

- Attend activities that are offered around mealtimes. Community events, potlucks, or home groups can provide alternatives to eating alone.

- Rearrange seating, change mealtime hours, or choose new ways to eat your meals. While it might be tempting to eat fast food and avoid mealtimes altogether, it is important to take care of yourself and eat healthy.

2. Buying Food

Even for a spouse who does not normally do the food shopping, going to a grocery store can cause feelings of aloneness when separated. Pushing a cart, wondering what to buy, and seeing items that their spouse enjoyed eating or cooking is just another reminder that there is someone missing at home. Store clerks, hoping to make friendly conversation, can spark sadness just by asking if you have got an exciting weekend planned.

Proactive Tips

- Since shopping for food is necessary, consider inviting someone along who is unable to drive and needs to shop regularly. If you have a willing teenager in your family who wants to practice driving, he or she might be happy for the opportunity to go anywhere with you. (The opportunity to talk with teens does not come along often and will be gone quickly.)

- Invite a friend or take a child along when you shop.

- Try shopping at different stores. If you have never gone to a whole-foods-type store, for instance, it can be interesting seeing food or toiletry items packaged in new ways. Try driving to a different area of town or even out of town to get items that will not spoil. You can use that time to sightsee, or window shop, just to change things up.

- If you have fallen into a rut of eating the same type of food every evening, try buying something different, or research new ways of barbequing meats and veggies. Spend a little more time in the produce department.

- Take a cooking class, and make new friends that you can go to dinner with or cook with (being careful to guard against relationships that could result in an emotional or sexual affair).

- If your spouse was the one who did all the shopping and cooking, and this is new territory for you, let this be a learning-and-stretching experience. (Your new talents will not go unnoticed.)

3. Evenings

Since most couples have evening routines which include spending time together, watching television, reading, playing games, and/or being intimate, evenings can be the loneliest of times when separated. Even when couples are in crisis, and some of the fun has already gone out of the marriage, there is still comfort knowing that there is another adult in the home when the day is over, and the lights go out.

As Michelle mentioned in her statement, even though you might be physically separated, you are still married in God's eyes. Being sexually intimate with an estranged spouse is not a sin, but it may send mixed messages if you or your spouse is unwilling to work towards reconciliation. In addition, if your spouse is intimately involved with another person, spending the night together will not help him or her to repent.

Proactive Tips

- If you tend to stay up late, go to bed earlier and read or watch a movie in bed. If you went to bed early, try staying up later. Add or take out a television just to change the atmosphere.

- Try taking a community course and use evenings to do homework.

- If you have children or family members who play sports, attending their games will not only get you out of the house, but provide support for them as well.

- Write, read, learn, spend time in God's Word, and let evenings be a time for you to fill your mind with new things that are spiritually and mentally healthy.

- Be social, but exercise self-control, and make wise decisions. Yes, you will feel lonely at times, but there are plenty of healthy activities you can do to fill your time.

Remaining faithful to a spouse who has left the marriage is not easy. It is painful. Still, God often uses pain to draw us near Him and make us stronger people. What many abandoned spouses don't take into consideration is that the husband or wife who left the marriage will experience loneliness too. As mentioned, even if there is a third party involvement, missing the spouse he or she left can actually help foster repentance and reconciliation, as long as the abandoned spouse is waiting.

LESSON ONE

Scripture Reading

Pray first, and read the following Scriptures. Read the surrounding verses, as well to help you with the context. Answer the questions on a separate piece of paper or in your journal if you need more room.

Read John 14:15-30 and answer the following questions:

1. In verse 15 Jesus says that if we love Him, we will do what?

2. In verse 16 Jesus promises us what?

3. In verse 18, what other promise does Jesus make?

4. In verse 21 Jesus says He will reveal Himself to whom?

5. In verse 23 Jesus promises that He and His Father will make a home where?

6. In verses 27-29 Jesus is leaving something the world cannot give us. What is it?

For You to Consider

List additional times that you tend to feel lonely. Based on the Scriptures and tips in this lesson, what can you do to face times of loneliness? If you are in a group, share your ideas together.

FINANCIAL STRAIN

Don't love money; be satisfied with what you have. For God said, 'I will never fail you. I will never abandon you.'

—

Hebrews 13:5

Money issues are often the source of quarrels between husbands and wives, but when a separation occurs, financial strain can happen even for couples who never had money problems. In fact, sometimes more money just means more strain. Regardless of your financial situation, you will want to be equipped to deal with challenges in this area. We have actually known couples who decided to do the hard work to save their marriage once they factored in the cost of getting a divorce. If you are already physically separated from your spouse, and he or she is willing to discuss this lesson with you, it would be beneficial, even if reconciliation were not on the horizon. If you have children, it is even more important to learn tools that can help you avoid overreacting and making financial decisions that will negatively affect the rest of your life.

Common Causes of Financial Strain When Physically Separated

1. Legal Fees

For most, by the time a physical separation occurs, there has been talk or threats of divorce. As a result, it is common for one or both spouses to seek legal advice in an effort to protect their assets. Oftentimes, this advice starts the ball rolling with legal fees that cause even more problems. We received a call from one lady who said she received a large bill in the mail after simply speaking to an attorney over the phone. She said, "I did not know that I would be charged for the phone call. When the bill came, it caused a huge argument between my husband and I, and we were already on shaky ground in our marriage!" In this lady's case, she and her husband decided to take a reconciliation class rather than spend money on attorney fees, and they are still together today.

Custody battles are another reason couples incur exorbitant legal bills. While child support laws are in place to help children, most kids just want their parents to stop fighting—especially when it involves them. Of course, sometimes legal fees are unavoidable, such as in life-threatening situations or crimes against children. Just do your best by practicing the following tips.

Proactive Tips

- Before you seek the advice of an attorney, try meeting with a mediator. Mediators know the law, but they don't do divorces. Reconciliation classes are available in many communities. (Visit our website for help in locating a class near you, or for information about our online classes.)

- If your spouse has already filed for a legal separation or divorce, do your best to be amiable, calm, and forgiving while waiting for God to work behind the scenes. It is always best to proceed with caution and stay focused on God. Consider the following analogy: Just as we have the right to proceed through a green light in an intersection, we may end up "dead right" if we don't stop for the person in the wrong who is running a red light. Read Philippians 4:13 and 19.

Even if you feel that you have the right to file for a divorce, think about waiting and doing nothing. This can be hard, but time is often our friend.

2. **Cost of Two Households**

Since a physical separation requires at least one spouse to move out, there is usually financial strain due to setting up an additional household. Regardless of the couple's financial status, having two households means less cash flow. When couples have separate households, it is especially difficult for families with children. There is double the cost for clothes, personal items, and furniture. Even for those who don't have children or whose children are adults, two households will always cost more than one.

Proactive Tips

- If your spouse was the one to move out of the home, and you are able to do so, consider renting out a room month to month, or for a season to a college student or same-gender person that is referred by a trusted source.

- By keeping the agreement month to month or seasonal, you will be able to have your spouse move back home in a timely manner when you reconcile. Some people advertise and rent to people who come to town on business. This can generate lucrative extra income if you are able.

- If you were forced to move from your home for financial or other reasons, it would be better to stay with a friend, relative, or rent a room instead of setting up a separate residence. This would also send the message to your spouse that you are not making permanent decisions but waiting to reconcile instead. Of course, if you have children, this is not as easy, but we have known several people who have been able to make it work.

- If moving in with a family member or renting a room is not possible, consider waiting before you spend too much money on a new residence. Waiting on God may mean waiting to have what you want and living with only what you need for a time. Your spouse may also need to see that he or she is creating a financial hardship by wanting to separate.

- Avoid credit card use if possible. We have known people who used their credit cards because it helped them feel good to buy new things when setting up a separate residence. Unfortunately, they were so far in debt within the first three months that their marriage problems were even worse when they decided to reconcile. One lady shared, "My husband was a penny pincher, and I was a spendthrift, so when we separated, I couldn't wait to be free of his financial thumb. Now I look back and realize that had we just attended a class on finances and budgeting together it would have saved us thousands of dollars and a lot of heartache. We have been reconciled for 5 years, and I am still paying off the debt from my credit card spree during our six month separation. Through the class we took on finances during our reconciliation process, we learned that our differences were a blessing and not a curse. Of course, we have worked hard on learning to balance and budget."

3. Lack of Combined Resources

When couples physically separate, the lack of combined resources is felt immediately. Groceries, automobile expenses, bank charges, credit card use, and eating out can result in one or both spouses experiencing extreme financial pressure. For couples with small children, childcare costs may have to be budgeted due to a parent who was normally available for the children's needs having to work outside the home.

Proactive Tips

- Consider attending a home-church or community group. Community groups, Bible studies, home groups, and special interest groups can usually be joined immediately. A healthy support system will usually help one another in times of trouble. Networking and sharing ideas can help you get creative financially.

- Consider partnering with others in order to purchase larger quantities of food and household items to share.

- Childcare, transportation, and other areas of need can often be combined with family members or friends.

Last, remember to think of your separation as temporary, rather than permanent. Please avoid joining a coed, divorce recovery, or singles group and guard against getting emotionally or intimately involved with someone. You never know what God is doing behind the scenes. Wait, be patient, and do your best to be content with the resources you presently have.

LESSON TWO

Scripture Reading

Pray first, and read Matthew 6:19-34 and answer the following questions on a separate page or in your journal if you need more room.

1. In verse 19, what does Jesus say not to do?

2. In verse 20, what does He say to do instead?

3. What does Jesus say our eyes represent in verse 22?

4. In verse 24, what does Jesus say we cannot do?

5. In verses 25-27, Jesus lays out reasons not to worry. What do you struggle with most in this list? How does He conclude the verses?

6. In the remaining verses, what do you take away?

For You to Consider

Make a list of every area of your life in which you are facing financial challenges. Use a separate sheet of paper for each area. On each page, write what you can do immediately and what will have to be done over a longer period of time. Pray over each page, and place them in a binder. Put the binder aside. Every week, for the next six weeks, review your pages, and make notes as to what has changed. You will see that some things will improve, some may get worse, and others will not even be of concern anymore.

LESSON TWO

When you see something that can be done during the week, do your best to accomplish it. For the financial challenges that you have no control over, pray, and let God work behind the scenes as you trust Him to meet your needs. Apply the verses you have read, review them often, and do your best to remember them in every decision.

BETRAYAL

If God is for us, who can ever be against us?

—

Romans 8:31

We receive calls and emails daily from people who are separated. For the abandoned spouse, feeling betrayed is at the forefront of most of their pain.

From Bob

I made a decision not to file for a legal separation or divorce, regardless of the fact that I had biblical grounds to do so. My wife left our marriage to date her boss, who was also married. One day, out of the blue, nearly four years later, my wife called and said she wanted to reconcile. I was a little apprehensive to move back together without counseling, so I recommended that we meet with a Christian counselor for at least three months. We were just about ready to move back together, when I discovered that she was secretly meeting with the man she had the affair with. I felt betrayed and disrespected, and our reconciliation abruptly came to an end. She ended up filing for a divorce soon after and they are now married. It seemed that her desire to reconcile was only to make him jealous so he would divorce his wife—which he did. While the four-year separation was hard, nothing compared to the betrayal I felt as a result of her manipulating tactics that finally ended our marriage.

From Marsha

My husband was emotionally involved with a lady he worked with when he told me he wanted to separate. It did not take long for the attraction to become a full-blown affair. I was shocked, because he never seemed the type of person who could do that. In all areas of his life he was loyal and believed in the importance of keeping his word. In the beginning I kept telling myself that he would change his mind and come back. I attended a class, read the Bible, and prayed. Sometimes it seemed that he was moving towards reconciliation; then, he would change his mind and go back to her. Finally, one year later, he left the lady and got his own place. When we started moving towards reconciliation, I was surprised to find that it wasn't as easy as I imagined it would be. The feelings of betrayal were so deep inside my heart, that the thought of trusting him again seemed impossible. We are still working on our marriage, but it has been a long road.

From Jan

When my husband moved out, I was eight-months pregnant with our fourth child, living a couple thousand miles away from my family. Substance abuse and infidelity were the main problems in our marriage. I had put off calling my family, hoping he would return to us and change his life. When I reached out to his family, who just lived a few miles from us, to my disappointment, they treated me as if it were my fault that he wasn't a better husband. My husband and his family's disloyal behavior left me no choice but to let my friends and family know what was going on. I felt embarrassed by being betrayed by my own husband. A few months later, I returned to my family for support. That was nearly three years ago, and my husband hasn't given up his lifestyle to work on our marriage. I still feel betrayed by him and his family, but I also feel thankful that God provided the support and loyalty that my children and I needed through my family.

When a marriage is in crisis, parents might side with their son or daughter's spouse in an attempt to help save the marriage. But once a physical separation occurs, it is common, such as with Jan's in-laws, for parents to side with their son or daughter, amplifying feelings of betrayal. In Jan's case, her marriage ended in an unwanted divorce even though she waited for her husband to repent and change his life. She focused on getting herself emotionally and spiritually healthy and on being the best mom she could be. Her parents created a safe support system, and she was able to live with them while going back to school. Even though Jan felt betrayed by her husband and his family, she did not use that as an excuse to feel abandoned and betrayed by God.

Common Times to Feel Betrayed

1. Special Occasions

Birthdays, anniversaries, holidays, or family gatherings are common times to experience the emotion of betrayal. Betrayal means to go against a promise. Each time you are reminded that your spouse has chosen to walk away from a promise to stay married it will be cause for this emotion to surface. With time it will lessen but in the beginning, it is very painful for most.

Proactive Tips

- There is a lot to be said about keeping family traditions when a separation takes place. However, traditions are going to be different regardless of how hard a spouse tries to keep things the same.

- It is helpful to remember that traditions are often thwarted even when couples have a great marriage. Illness, tragedies, unexpected events, or change of income can cause families to stop the normal way of doing things.

- Life is rarely consistent. Change is a part of living, and when we can learn to embrace change, it is better for everyone, especially children.

- Avoid being a victim at all costs. Not only is it more difficult on loved ones to see you suffering over broken traditions, but it is also unappealing. Some people tend to play the victim card in hopes of making their spouse feel sorry and return home. Making someone feel guilty for your sadness will end up doing just the opposite.

- Look ahead and make a plan as to how you can embrace the change that is coming. If you have children, this is especially important. For instance, birthdays can be handled by planning to have two celebrations if necessary.

- If you and your spouse are on friendly terms, see if he or she will discuss some options. (Understand that this is not typical in the first few months, but if your separation is lasting longer, some couples are able to do this.)

- If your spouse is not being cooperative, make plans now as to how you can help your child or family members experience birthdays or holidays that will avoid creating conflict between you and your spouse.

However you choose to deal with special occasions, doing so with a good attitude will help you avoid feelings of betrayal and go a long way towards reconciliation.

2. Church Gatherings

Many separated people have said that attending church, Bible studies, or any function at church was difficult, especially in the beginning. When couples split, it often creates uncomfortable feelings of allegiance for their friends. Invitations to events are often not sent in order to avoid choosing which person to invite. It is awkward for all people involved, regardless of who initiated the separation. Couples who are separated do not necessarily stop attending church, so it can create uneasy feelings when they both attend the same service. Abandoned spouses are forced to put on a brave face while suffering on the inside, watching seemingly happy couples sit together.

It can also be embarrassing, regardless of which role you have played in your separation. One man shared, "I was the one who moved out, but people did not know the whole story. They did not know that my wife had been seeing another man, and when I gave her an ultimatum, she chose him. I was embarrassed to talk about my problems with others, so I started attending a church where people did not know us. Some time has passed now, but every once in a while I wish I had been brave enough to face the humiliation and continued attending that church."

Proactive Tips

- Continue to attend or start attending a church. Even though attending church may trigger feelings of betrayal, it is also a place where you can create the kind of spiritual and emotional support system you need. It is most important to connect with people of all ages, in all walks of life, who will help hold you accountable to godly principles. The worst thing you can do is to be alone, away from others, feeling sad and betrayed. Jesus knew betrayal above all else. But even in the midst of His greatest pain of being betrayed by one of His disciples, Jesus continued to fellowship and break bread with those He loved. Yes, He went away alone to pray often, but He also modeled the importance of being with others.

- Avoid attending a co-ed singles group. Sometimes Christians can be insensitive when it comes to embracing people who are separated from their spouse. On the other extreme, there are those in the church that promote separated people into a singles ministry. Separated people are NOT single. They are separated, and separation is a no-man's land: no longer living with a spouse, but not free to date or remarry. No doubt, being separated is emotionally painful.

- Allow God to work behind the scenes with your spouse. Protect your heart from becoming hard or bitter, so that you can be ready to reconcile when the time comes.

3. Bedtime

It is not uncommon for couples who are in crisis to experience feelings of betrayal at bedtime, even prior to a physical separation. The difference for someone who is separated, however, is that the abandoned spouse is not sure what their absent spouse is doing at bedtime. Thoughts often run rampant as to where, with whom, or what is going on when the lights go out. A quiet, dark, empty home can be an invitation to thoughts and fears we never think about during the day.

Proactive Tips

- Your thoughts in the evening can be your worst enemy. Jesus said to dwell on things that are good. Memorize Scriptures and read something positive when you get in bed.

- If you are living in the home you shared with your spouse, consider moving to a different bedroom or completely redecorating the one you are in. We have known several widows or widowers who did this, and it was a big help. Also consider changing the time you go to bed. As mentioned in an earlier lesson, if you tend to go to bed late, go earlier, and vice versa.

- Consider writing a note and framing it in your bedroom that reads: God will never leave me, and while I might *feel* alone, I am *not* alone.

From Mary Lynn

Even though I initiated the separation by telling my husband to leave, I felt abandoned by my husband and by God when I asked my husband to return home, and he refused. I was filled with anxiety and was panic-stricken once I realized he might not ever return. I couldn't sleep and was exhausted. I was ready to give up on life, and everything was crashing down around me. I had thought my relationship with God was strong, but now I realize I had been relying on myself. Through my obedience in attending church, taking the reconciliation classes, and getting into a support group my relationship grew deeper. He is now my peace. He is my joy. He is my life.

LESSON THREE

Mary Lynn's testimony is in the introduction of this book. As mentioned, she is continuing to wait on God's timing and believes she and her husband will reconcile one day. Her testimony is a good example of how church and fellowship with other believers can sustain someone who feels hopeless and help them grow in their spiritual maturity.

LESSON THREE

Scripture Reading

Pray first and read John 17:20-25 and John 18:1-36, including surrounding passages if you aren't familiar with these verses. Answer the following questions:

1. In verse 20, whom did Jesus say He was praying for?

2. In verses 21-23, what did He pray we would do?

3. In verses 25-26 what did Jesus say about the disciples?

4. In Chapter 18, verse 2 what was Judas called?

5. In verse 36, what does Jesus say about His Kingdom?

For You to Consider

Based on the Scriptures you just read, discuss or write in your journal what Jesus must have gone through when he was betrayed. It is never too late to commit or recommit our life to Christ. Take time this week to think about your commitment to the Lord, and how you can be a better follower of Jesus by obeying Him in all areas of your life. Talk with your support group or accountability partner about any area of your life that you feel needs to be changed.

LACK OF PURPOSE

"For I know the plans that I have for you," says the Lord. "They are plans for good and not for disaster, to give you a future and a hope.

—

Jeremiah, 29:11

The ripping apart of a marriage is painful on all levels, and it is one reason God hates divorce. If you are currently experiencing a lack of purpose for your life because of a choice your spouse made, please don't give up. Your role as a husband or wife is only a portion of who you are. There is hope. While some people marry because they don't want to be alone, many marry because they want to share life's experiences with another person. They find purpose in giving up a part of themselves for their family and being less self-focused. They enjoy the role of wife, husband, or parent, and for them, they find purpose through sacrificing some of their wants in order to meet the needs of others. We receive emails and calls regularly from people who have fallen into depression because of losing their lack of purpose.

From Patrick

When my wife left and took our four children, my life fell apart. Looking back now, it is easy to see how I could have done things differently, but when our separation first happened, I did not do very well. Each minute that went by, when there was no contact from my wife, seemed like hours. Now I realize that God works things out in His time, His way. I was used to being a husband and a dad, and my selfish human desires for the relationship to be restored caused me to react in ways I wish I hadn't done. Even when I thought I was putting God first in my life, it was really only a token gesture. But months later, I remember clearly lying in bed one night, realizing God was finally at the center of my life, and not my wife anymore. This is not something I believed would ever happen. I had purpose again.

LESSON FOUR

Common Times for Feeling a Lack of Purpose

1. When Planning Your Future

Regardless of your age, or how long you have been married, it is natural for you and your spouse to discuss the future together. We are all wired to think about tomorrow, next week, next year, and beyond. The beginning of a separation has been described as "floating on an ocean that has no shore in sight." You know you are going somewhere, but you don't know when or how the voyage will end. When your mind begins to think about the future, it is impossible to plan because you are unsure in so many areas of your life. This is an area that can affect your whole family, and you must learn to stay focused and purposed.

Proactive Tips

- Tell yourself the truth: your future is on hold, but you will get through this time. Denial will only lead you to take matters into your own hands, believing that doing something is better than doing nothing.

- Don't fall into the trap of believing that dating or filing for divorce can help you "move on" and find purpose again. Live in the truth and trust God.

- Help others in need. When your thoughts turn to concerns about your future, ask God to show you something that needs to be done for someone else TODAY. There is always someone in need. If you have children or grandchildren, you will not have to look very far. God's purposes are usually centered on helping others in some way. If you ask, He will show you. There may be someone in your church or community that can plug you into a non-profit organization that can use help. Many of our volunteers are people who felt their purpose in life was on hold during their separation.

- Set short-term goals for getting away. Even though your long-term future is on hold while you are separated, this does not mean that you can't set short-term goals and have fun. If you have children in the home, make plans for a family get-a-way. Get creative, and look for ways the whole family can earn extra money. Getting away does not have to mean a costly vacation. It can be something as simple as taking a drive to the mountains, lake or beach, to fish, or gather items for making gifts. If you are alone, consider setting a time to visit a friend or family member. Set goals that are achievable and not costly, which allow you to get out of your regular routine and environment.

2. Lack or Change of Obligations

Fill your free time constructively. Some people have difficulty adjusting to the fact that they no longer need to fill the needs or wants of their spouse. This is especially true for a wife or husband who has been in business or ministry together. Even for those whose spouse was demanding, many admit that experiencing free time for the first time was hard.

Proactive Tips

- Budget your time. Make a list of your current daily obligations. Don't think about what you had prior to the separation; only consider what you have now. Some people find that they have less free time, due to picking up the slack of their spouse not helping out. If that's the case for you, decide which obligations you can delegate or give up. (Your friends and family will understand if you let them know that you are making changes in order for you to stay rested and healthy.)

- Take on new obligations. If you have more free time, consider taking on new obligations. This will take planning, but finding purpose comes when we are equipped to handle the time God has given us to manage. Balance is the key.

From Jim

When my wife and I separated, I went through a tough time, even though I was the one who walked out in the middle of an argument. She is a type "A" personality, and I am laid back. Most of our arguments were over her being too busy, while I wanted to stay home and rest. We weren't separated all that long. To my surprise, I actually missed her "to-do" lists and having a purposeful life. When got back together, we made an agreement to be easy on each other. She lets me rest, and I don't complain when I get a list of things to do. We learned to compromise, and our reconciliation has worked.

From Teresa

When I first attended the reconciliation group in my community, I met a woman who had been separated for two years. I had only been separated for seven months. I told myself that there was no way I was waiting two years! My husband wasn't interested in getting counseling, and he was moving further from the marriage. Through my accountability and prayer group, I stayed focused, even though there were times that I wanted to just move on. After a year, I did not feel that I was doing anything constructive with my life. Most of my time was spent feeling sorry for myself instead of being productive. Finally, I reasoned that if I was going to be stuck in "limbo-land", at least I could be doing something with all my free time. So, I decided to go back to school. My husband still hasn't returned home, but he hasn't filed for divorce either. The funny thing is that now we have been separated for over two years, but the waiting hasn't been as bad as I thought. I have stayed busy with school, and still hold on to hope that we will reconcile. Recently, my husband mentioned counseling. My verse is, "...with God all things are possible," from Matthew 19:26. My life is full of purpose and hope, because I have learned to trust God and lean on Him, regardless of what happens in my marriage.

3. When Others Ask Questions

Questions simply meant to start conversations can do just the opposite. For example, if you have been struggling with a lack of purpose, a friendly bank teller or grocery clerk asking how your day has been can make you feel worse and want to clam up. Even well-meaning family members and friends can ask questions about your future that may cause you to feel a lack of purpose. Being prepared with responses that are truthful and pre-planned can help you avoid being caught off-guard and coming across defensively or hopeless.

Proactive Tips

- Assume the best from others. Realize that every store clerk, greeter, and agency teller is told to be friendly. They aren't being nosey (although it feels that way at times), and they ask everyone similar questions.

- Have pre-planned answers. You can have an answer ready that leaves out details, and yet is polite, such as, "For now, I am not sure, but thanks for asking."

- Avoid shutting people out just because you feel discouraged with a life that seems to be on hold. The truth is that when people ask questions, many do so just to have something to say. Share as much as you feel like sharing, but don't let people pressure you into talking about details if you don't feel like talking, or don't have an answer. At the end of the day, it is important to feel good about your interaction with others, and let God allow those interactions to glorify Him.

From Patrick

When my wife left—pride was a huge issue as it was her call to separate. I pretty much hid away from everyone for three to four weeks. If I did bump into anyone, I tried to put on a brave face, but this was only possible for a certain length of time. My wife was telling everyone that she wanted a divorce, and I couldn't hide any longer. My pastor helped me with what to tell people since we had both been involved at our church. The script we came up with was along the lines of, "We are currently having a few difficulties and we are trying to work them out, but until we manage to resolve them we are separated." While this line was horrible for me to say, at least I was answering the questions, and I felt I wasn't being rude. I needed the support of others during that time more than I thought. When I stopped hiding from them, it helped with my spiritual health as well.

Even people who are happily married can struggle with a sense of purpose if he or she is too focused on their spouse to provide it. Life's journey is full of changes which will require each of us to find purpose in every turn of events. The only way to find real purpose is to keep an eternal perspective on life and allow God to be in every decision.

LESSON FOUR

Scripture Reading

Pray first, and read the following Scriptures. Read the surrounding verses, as well to help you with the context. Answer the questions on a separate piece of paper or in your journal, if you need more space.

1. 1 Corinthians 9:24-26

   • What does Paul compare purpose to?

   • Why do you think Paul associated purpose with discipline?

2. Philippians 2:1-5

   • Paul's letter to the Christians in Philippi was to encourage them during a difficult time. He did not want them to feel that their persecution was without purpose. What did he say would make him happy in these verses?

   • In verse 4, did Paul say that we are not to care for ourselves? What did he assume we would do naturally?

   • Do you think someone without purpose is taking care of their own interests?

3. 2 Timothy 2:3-7

   • What is Paul telling Timothy to do and how do these verses tie in with the example in 1 Corinthians?

For You to Consider

What do you think Paul would say to you if you could have a conversation with him today? What tips do you plan to implement as a result of this lesson?

VULNERABILITY

God is never tempted to do wrong, and He never tempts anyone else. Temptation comes from our own desires, which entice us and drag us away.

—

James 1:13-14

Regardless of who initiates the separation, once a couple no longer lives together, both can become vulnerable to desires that can cause irreparable damage to their marriage. In addition to adultery, addictions such as gambling, sexual, substance abuse, credit card use, and much more can hinder reconciliation. For the person who initiates the separation, it is not uncommon to self-sabotage their imagined "new beginning" because of guilt. While it is never too late to repent and turn to God, self-destructive behavior may result in it being too late to return to a spouse. If you are tempted to do anything that can be self-destructive, stop. You may be tempted to stay in bed all day rather than go to work or school, or give in to actions of rage even though that may be the very excuse your spouse used for leaving in the first place. The definition of "vulnerable" is to be easily persuadable or liable to give in to temptation. It is important to remember that you are in a spiritual war as much as an emotional one if your spouse is refusing to work towards reconciliation. Even so, there is hope. God loves marriage, and He will equip you to win over any temptation, as long as you focus on Him.

From Chuck

My wife and I were separated for eight months and have been reconciled now for more than fifteen years. I was tired of our arguing, so I packed a few clothes and went to my hometown, a couple of hundred miles away, just for a change of view. I planned to stay a week or so, but once I got around my old drinking buddies, I got back into some old habits that were not good. This made my wife so angry that she filed for a legal separation and threatened to fight for custody of our young son. My behavior resulted in our separation lasting much longer than it needed to. Instead of me being able to return home, I had to get an apartment and do a lot of work to win her back. Whenever I talk to a guy who thinks he can move out of his home, just to get some time to think or take a break from his family without falling into bad behavior, I tell him otherwise. I almost lost my family.

From Carole

I told my husband to move out when he discovered that I was having an affair. Even though I repented and broke off the affair a week later, my husband refused to reconcile. Not long after we separated, my husband started dating and living as though he were single. He used the discovery of my unfaithfulness as an excuse to do whatever he pleased. When I was at my lowest point, I got an email response from a reconciliation ministry leader, with contact information for a woman in my area, who was offering a small group in her home. I did my best from that time on to follow the principles in the ministry. I changed jobs, in order to avoid all contact with the person I'd had the affair with. I also limited any time alone with men and attended church regularly. Obviously, our marriage had a lot of problems, but I regret running to the arms of another man for solace. Who knows how things would have played out if I'd suggested counseling to my husband, instead of asking him to leave our home?

Boundaries are important in marriage but even more so when a couple is separated. Be prepared in this area, and protect your relationship with God and with your spouse. Avoid being vulnerable, and be ready to reconcile.

Common Causes for Vulnerability

1. Improper Boundaries with the Opposite Sex

Healthy boundaries should be implemented in the workplace and public settings, including church. Many mistakenly believe that church is a safe place to let their guard down with the opposite sex. If you are a friendly person by nature and don't mind giving hugs and talking with people, you may end up sending the wrong signal. Friendliness can often be misunderstood. When a person is separated, they need to avoid becoming a target for people who may not be spiritually mature enough to realize that separation is not divorce. A separated person is still married and should be off limits to flirting and being asked for dates.

Proactive Tips

- Set boundaries in co-ed support groups or Bible studies. Try to share your personal struggles with same-gender attendees. In a church setting, or when praying in a small group, try to hold hands of same-gender people if possible. It is hard to believe, but we have spoken with people who admitted that their affair began when holding the hand of a caring person, of the opposite sex, who simply wanted to pray with them.

- Remember that you are in a spiritual warfare in your marriage. Create a same-gender accountability prayer group that you can email or talk with weekly.

- Avoid having close friends of the opposite sex. It may sound rigid, but what is it worth to protect your heart and someone else's?

- Meet in groups of three or more when doing church or work activities in co-ed settings.

- Avoid going to lunch or coffee with someone of the opposite sex, even if it is to talk about work or ministry. Ask their spouse or a friend to join you.

- Identify an attraction and flee. If you find yourself thinking, "I am looking forward to seeing this person again. I feel alive. I don't want to reconcile with my spouse anymore," think twice. Are you trusting God, or, are you relying on your emotions? We become vulnerable when we shift our thinking from reconciling to moving on and letting someone else move in to our heart. It is never easy to flee the presence of someone who makes you feel good, but you must do so if you want to avoid falling in love with someone while you are still married.

2. Settings That Trigger Addiction Issues

If you have struggled with any type of addictions in the past, they can pop up again simply because you have no one to hold you accountable anymore. As mentioned, addictions might include behaviors such as, overuse of charge cards, gambling, substance abuse, pornography, or anything that is done to extreme, which is considered sinful behavior in God's Word. One man shared that he couldn't even drive in the direction of a casino that was two hours away, since it would trigger his habit of a gambling addiction. Some people have shared that sexual behaviors they thought were long gone resurfaced when their spouse was no longer in the home or helping them be accountable.

Proactive Tips

- Don't isolate. Having a roommate or children in the home can be a tremendous help to avoid isolation. If you were the one who moved out, hopefully you are in a temporary setting with a friend or relative. If not, consider taking in a roommate. Just having someone else to talk with and ask questions can be a safety mechanism to protect you from falling when tempted.

- Many people have shared that they joined or rejoined an addiction recovery group. This is helpful if you find yourself giving in to behaviors or thoughts that you can't seem to control. If the group is a faith-based group, it is especially helpful.

- Same-gender Bible studies are helpful. Just having somewhere to go weekly, with people who share healthy values and lifestyles, will help protect you against being vulnerable.

- Memorize Scripture, and use it. Bad habits are hard to break, but with practice and God's help, you can do it.

3. Arguing with Your Spouse

While it is important to spend time with your spouse if you want to reconcile, you must avoid arguing or abusing one another. Doing so will simply provide excuses as to why you should file for divorce and "move on." If your spouse is being physically intimate with someone else or is physically or verbally abusive, it will be more difficult to have adult conversations that can foster a climate of reconciliation. Even couples who have reconciled say that it was difficult in the beginning to learn to have healthy conversations. One couple shared, "When we used to meet during the first year of our separation, it always resulted in a heated argument. This would set us back and further away from reconciliation. Then a friend suggested that we meet in public places to discuss hot topics. We started meeting in restaurants, and that worked for us. Because we had to keep our voices down, and it was more difficult to walk away, we learned good habits that we continue to use today."

It is important to find what will work in your particular situation. Some people talk better in a confined space, while others need the freedom to walk away when the conversation goes south. Practice the suggested tips, and don't be afraid to try something new. It is probably safe to say that whatever you and your spouse have been doing has not worked.

Proactive Tips

- Some couples have discovered that when discussing important issues, going for a walk helps.

- Test different methods of communicating. One man shared that he can talk with his wife on the phone, but texting or emailing does not work: "She tends to misunderstand me when I text or email. She tells me that my words come across harsh, so I make sure that I call or see her in person when I want to talk about something important." Other people have shared that text messages or emails are better received by their spouse.

- If you and your spouse are on friendly enough terms, going for a drive can be a good way to talk. While one person may feel trapped in a car, another might enjoy knowing that their spouse can't just walk away when discussing important issues. Concerning Joe and Michelle's separation, Joe said, "At the end of our separation, we had started talking civil to each other. So, we took a day trip about an hour and a half away, and it was on that trip, in the car, that we ended up talking about the issues that Michelle said she had been waiting to discuss for almost two years. Maybe it was that neither of us could walk away, or that I was focused on driving and just talked naturally with her. All I know is that having time alone in that car was what we needed. We moved back together that weekend."

Whatever you can do to make your discussions less explosive, do so. It is important to create a safe place where each of you can say what's on your mind in a way that is respectful. Protect yourself at all cost from feeling discouraged and hopeless each time you speak to your spouse. There is always hope as long as God is at the center, because He wants the best for you.

LESSON FIVE

Scripture Reading

Pray first, and read the following Scriptures. Read the surrounding verses, to help you with the context. Answer the questions on a separate piece of paper or in your journal, if you need more space.

1. Read Matthew 18:7

    - What does Jesus say about temptation?

    - What does He say about the one who causes the temptation?

    - Have you ever thought about the role you play in someone else's life concerning temptation?

2. Read Luke 4:1-2

    - What was Jesus' condition when He was tempted?

    - What was He full of, and what did He lack?

    - How do you think our spiritual and physical condition sets us up for success or failure when tempted?

3. Read 1 Corinthians 10:12-13. People often misquote these verses and say that God does not give us more than we can handle, but that is nowhere in Scripture. We certainly *do* get more than we can handle, but what the Scripture does teach is that we are never tempted beyond what we can handle. What do these verses tell you about temptation? What will happen if we focus on God when tempted?

4. Read James 1:12-15. These are important verses concerning temptation. Please read each verse carefully, and answer the questions.

  • Verse 12: What does God do if we pass the test when tempted?:

  • Verse 13: What are we not supposed to say when tempted?:

  • Verse 14: Where does temptation come from?:

  • Verse 15: What happens if we give in?:

For You to Consider

This lesson is extremely important, not just for your marriage, but for your own personal journey. How do you tend to deal with temptation? If you aren't in an accountability group, or have an accountability partner, you will be less likely to stand against temptation.

ALIENATION

Let all that I am wait quietly before God, for my hope is in Him. He alone is my rock and my salvation, my fortress where I will not be shaken.

—

Psalm 62:5-6

God created humans with a desire to connect with others. Some people thrive in crowds of people, while others prefer one-on-one interaction. No one wants to be alone all of the time. Most would agree that solitary confinement is among the cruelest of punishments. When a couple physically separates, even the spouse who initiated the separation can find him or herself struggling with the emotional pain of alienation. We have known of couples who decided to get marital help simply because one or both spouses missed the togetherness of family or social gatherings.

This lesson is not about feeling lonely, as discussed in Lesson One. It is more about feeling so disconnected from a loved one or community that it triggers an emotion of fear or panic. It is similar to the feeling a small child has when separated from their mom or dad in a large crowd. We all have a sense of community within our workplace, church, or family, which helps us not feel alone in the universe. When this community is disrupted, and one or both people feel alienated, it can lead to hopelessness.

Alienation can also trigger feelings of insecurity or unworthiness. Most of us have childhood memories of waiting to be chosen for a sports team, dance partner, or activity, hoping not to be the last person standing. Feelings of insecurity and unworthiness are not from God. God created us with a purpose, and with unique gifts and talents to be used with and for others.

From James

> *My wife and I separated more than once. Each time she would return to her parents with the children, and they would surround her and not let me near. The last time we separated she sought legal advice, and the wall became like a cocoon that was impenetrable. She still attended our church but did not want to go to the same service I attended. I was not physically abusive to her, but she had accused me of being emotionally abusive, and as*

a result, many of our previous friends and her family pushed me away too. Even though it looked hopeless, I tried to hold on. The holidays were the most difficult, but I continued to pray for restoration even though it was the loneliest time of my life. We were separated for over a year, and I don't think I could have made it without the support from a few people who reached out and made me attend family gatherings and social functions. I wanted to sit in the dark and brood, but they wouldn't let me. I'm grateful that I did not give in to the negative feelings and fears. Even though we have been reconciled for over five years, I can still remember how it felt to be alone during that time.

Common Reasons for Feeling Alienated

1. When a Marriage is in Crisis

Once couples in crisis begin to use the words "separation" or "divorce" behind closed doors, one spouse can start excluding the other from things such as, family gatherings, work parties, or church-related events. Not always, but in some cases, this alienation is created to make a separation easier.

It is also common in many crisis marriage situations, for the person who is most unhappy to create an atmosphere in the home that fosters alienation rather than togetherness. He or she may make excuses for not coming home right after work, going to bed alone, or not eating meals together. For the spouse who is being ignored, it is especially difficult because alienation creates distrust and a fear of abandonment for many. Trying to communicate their frustrations often makes matters worse, and the emotional pain of feeling pushed away just escalates.

Proactive Tips

- If you have been separated for three months or more, you have probably already experienced the alienation stage that many crisis couples go through. If this is the case, be comforted in knowing that God went before you to create the support and resources that you now have.

- Pray and ask your spouse if he or she is willing to talk about how you both are feeling. Avoid threatening or accusing your spouse in any way. Just explain that you are feeling alienated and provide some reasons as to why. After you have addressed the issue, let it go for a while.

- Along with the Bible, begin reading books that will help you focus on God and not your spouse.

- Create space. Smothering your spouse, because you feel alienated, rarely works. Giving your spouse space may be difficult—especially if he or she is already pulling away—but it is better than begging for the attention you are craving.

- The best results come when the person feeling alienated speaks truth and behaves in an adult manner. Self-respect is most important. Thinking back to our school days, we would probably all agree that the people who seemed to never be left out were the ones who did not care if they were.

2. Initial Stages of Separation

Feeling alienated from everyone—including God—is one of the first emotions for an abandoned spouse to experience. In the initial stages of a separation, we believe that there is a window of time that church leaders, friends, and family members have to provide the help and hope this person needs.

We refer to the initial stages of separation as a twenty-four-hour to six-month timeframe. The first twenty-four hours are the most crucial because that is when emotions are highest in both spouses. We have even known of instances when couples decided to get counseling instead of separating because of a right response from caring family or friends. Even if you are not in the initial stages of your separation, these tips can still be helpful.

Proactive Tips

- Be still and listen. Even if the first twenty-four hour window of time has been lost, it is still not too late to react properly. Once your spouse sees you being mature, he or she will begin testing the waters to see if civil dialogue can occur. This is not to say that your spouse will always be civil, but at least you can model it first.

- Be the one to set the stage. Lasting reconciliation will only take place between two adults seeking God's will and doing what is right. It only takes one person to begin the process.

- Be around people. There is always a Bible study, support group, or community class available. Avoid feeling isolated from people. As mentioned in previous lessons, taking a class or joining an accountability group is important for many reasons, including not letting feelings of alienation take over.

3. When You Suspect, or Discover an Emotional or Physical Affair

Not always, but often, when a man or woman walks out on their spouse, there is already someone else in the wings. Many times it is an emotional attraction to someone that fuels the desire to separate in order to avoid feelings of guilt when he or she begins openly dating and becoming sexually intimate. For the abandoned spouse, just suspecting or knowing that their husband or wife has been emotionally connected with another can cause intense feelings of alienation. Once sexual intimacy is evident, the alienated spouse has to cope with even more emotional pain.

Proactive Tips

- If you don't know for certain that your spouse is having an affair (emotional or sexual), do not falsely accuse him or her. Doing so causes tempers to flair, and feelings of alienation will grow even more.

- If you discover that your spouse is in fact having an affair, you will need to get a support system in place immediately. In their book, *Yes, Your Marriage Can Be Saved*, Joe and Michelle discuss how to create a safe support system in Chapter Two.

- Be patient. Feelings of alienation will not subside for a while, but as long as you have the support to get through the initial stages after discovery, accountability will help you to avoid making decisions that you may regret later. It is hard to believe that marriages can be saved once adultery has occurred, but it happens more often than you think. Many couples who have survived adultery don't feel comfortable openly sharing it. Don't lose hope.

- Speak truth to your spouse. If your spouse refuses to discuss the area of unfaithfulness, continue speaking truth. Here is an example of what you might say: "I am disappointed that you are unwilling to discuss this important matter. At some point, the truth will come out, and I hope you are the one to tell me." Whatever you do, remain adult, and turn your focus to God. Get support, pray, and read Scripture.

- Trust God to bring truth to the light eventually. If you ask your spouse, "Is there someone else?" you will get an answer (even silence is an answer). The answer you get may not be the truth, but at least you have asked. You will eventually know for sure. Let it go, if you don't have proof that your spouse is being unfaithful. Truth will always come to light, eventually. We see it happen all the time. God often reveals truth once He has connected the person who is seeking truth to the support he or she will need.

From Patty

I suspected that my husband was having an affair, but he denied it each time I asked. He was in business with his father, and even he suspected that my husband was being unfaithful. Finally, in desperation, I hired a private investigator. My suspicions were confirmed when I learned that he was meeting with another woman after work regularly. When I confronted him with the evidence, he denied having a sexual affair. He tried to say that he and the woman were just good friends. When he refused to give up the "friendship," I filed for a divorce. I wasn't surprised to find that they moved in together soon after I filed. This was a few years ago, and he has not married the other woman. I guess there is a chance we could reconcile, but it will be hard. I don't think I could ever trust him with my heart again. His deception and pushing me away created intense feelings of isolation and pain, even if he wasn't being sexually intimate with her in the beginning.

Feelings of alienation may happen even if you reconcile. Some couples decide to stay married for the sake of their children, finances, or other reasons. While it is possible to be content and even happy in a marriage of convenience, many of these spouses admit that they feel alone. It takes work on both parts for a couple to create an atmosphere of togetherness in the home, but it is worth it. It will be important to address underlying issues and keep honest communication in your marriage in order to create true intimacy ("in-to-me-see").

LESSON SIX

Scripture Reading

Pray first, and read the following Scriptures. Read the surrounding verses, to help you with the context. Answer the questions on a separate piece of paper or in your journal if you need more space.

1. Read 2 Corinthians 4:7-9 and 16-17

Paul is telling the people in Corinth that his ministry is dedicated to equipping them to live without fear of death. Death is the ultimate alienation, unless we have the assurance that we will spend eternity with God and see our loved ones again. These verses are meant to address fear of physical death, and Paul has put truth to that fear.

- In verse 7, what does Paul compare our bodies to?

- Where does the power come from?

- In verses 8-9, what does Paul say happens to humans, and what NEVER happens?

- In verse 16, what does Paul tell the Corinthians is being renewed every day because he never gives up?

- In verse 17, what does Paul say about his present troubles?

2. Read 2 Corinthians 4:18 and Hebrews 13:4-6.

- In verse 4:18, Paul gives instructions to the Corinthians as to how to face troubles. Apply those instructions to your own life. What do these instructions say?

- In Hebrews 13, the writer gives practical instructions to followers of Christ. What do these verses say about marriage? What do they say about money?

- What does the writer of Hebrews say about God? Why do we never have to fear?

For You to Consider

If you feel alienated because of your spouse's choices to not obey God, what do you plan to do based on the tips and Scriptures in this lesson?

Final thought: If you love God and love others, you will never be alienated.

LESSON SEVEN

UNHEALTHY FEAR

*Do not be afraid or discouraged, for the Lord will personally go ahead
of you. He will be with you; He will neither fail you nor abandon you.*

—

Deuteronomy 31:8

Fear is an emotion that God gave us. He also created our bodies with the
ability to release adrenaline when we are afraid, and this hormone gives
us the physical strength to fight or flee from danger. However, not all fear
is healthy. Worry and anxiety caused by fears that are imagined or
unfounded are unhealthy. We refer to this type of fear as, "False
Evidences Appearing Real." When couples separate, one or both spouses
can experience unhealthy fears, such as, worry of what the future might
hold, or imagining the worst as to what their spouse will do. This lesson
will help you to be prepared and productive when living with unhealthy
fears. Regardless of what happens in your marriage, it is important to live
a productive life—especially if you have children or others who depend on
you.

Common Examples of Living With Unhealthy Fears

1. Isolating From Others

To be alone is not a bad thing. In fact, Jesus went away from the crowds
often to be alone. However, isolating from others is different than taking
time to be alone. Alienation, as discussed in the previous lesson, has to
do with people pushing you away. Isolation has to do with you pushing
people away.

If you are reading this lesson and thinking, "I don't want to be around
others," maybe you are too angry, hurt, embarrassed, or confused to be
around people. When we hurt, it is hard to think about anything other than
our own pain. God uses our pain to create a need, and He fills that need
through people. Take the time you need, but be careful that your
unhealthy fear of facing others in the midst of your pain does not result in
your being unproductive. Isolation is not just about you pushing others
away; it is also about not allowing God to use you to help others who are
hurting.

From Michelle

When Joe and I separated, our son was six years old and attended Christian school. I was embarrassed to be around the other moms because they all seemed so happily married. I no longer felt comfortable around them. I did not feel judged, but I felt pitied. As a result, I found myself making excuses for not attending anything that had to do with our son's school. Sadly, in an attempt to isolate myself from people who I thought pitied me, I missed out on social activities that would have also benefited our son. I avoided most of these moms the whole time that Joe and I were separated. When we reconciled, I realized that the very people I was staying away from were the ones who needed me as much as I needed them! When we started serving in ministry together, many of them approached me and said they had wanted to share their own marriage crises with me, but I wouldn't let them in.

Proactive Tips

- Attend church or support groups even if you prefer to be "alone with God." There is no doubt that you will need to spend more time alone with God. Everyone who has reached out to us for help during their separation, has agreed that their crisis was the catalyst that drove them into God's Word and prayer, but be a part of corporate worship or a support group as well.

- Accept invitations to social events. It is important to enjoy life, even if you would prefer to hide from others and stay home. Socializing will help you be more productive as you network with others in your community.

- Ask for prayer or support from people you trust. Sure, there are people who border on gossip when they share a prayer request or the latest news with too many details, but for the most part people do care. Give others the benefit of the doubt, and don't isolate yourself from the support many caring people would like to offer. You only need one or two people to make a difference.

2. Fear of Being Alone

The opposite of isolation is a fear of being alone. When a separation happens, it can cause or trigger "fear of abandonment" issues. We hear from men and women both who have had to learn to cope with this unhealthy fear. While this fear is unhealthy, it is real, and these tips can help.

Proactive Tips

- Consider getting an animal. A dog, cat, or even a bird can fill the void of feeling alone and give you purpose.

- Fill your home with music. While some songs may cause unwanted memories, other songs can do the opposite. Positive music can fill our minds with thoughts of God or pleasant memories. Learn to play a musical instrument, if you don't already do so. Many people have said that their most creative pieces happened as a result of feeling sad.

- Take up a new hobby or change careers. If you are afraid of being alone, fill your time doing something new. If you have ever considered changing careers or taking up a hobby, make the time to do so.

- Face your fear. Most people admit that facing their fears cured them of living with unhealthy fear. If you fear being alone, face it by implementing whatever tip you think will help. Discuss your fear of abandonment or being alone with someone you trust, and press on. With God at your side you are never alone, even though you may think you are.

From Marc

My drinking and alcoholic behavior drove my wife and three children out of our home for nearly a year. When they left to stay with her parents, I freaked out. I had no idea that their leaving would impact me like it did. Even though I was 32 years old at the time, I was actually afraid to be alone. I was willing to do whatever it took to get my family back home. My wife finally agreed to come home, if I would get help for my drinking problem. The recovery program that I joined also addressed my fear of abandonment and controlling behavior. I learned that the very thing I feared the most was what I put in motion by my self-destructive behavior. Had I not gotten help, I don't know where I'd be today. It for sure wouldn't be with my family.

3. Replacing Relationships With Work

Naturally, when a couple separates, there is financial strain and possibly a need for longer hours on the job. The fear of not having enough money can be overwhelming. If you find that your financial fear is causing you to work so much that you don't have time for relationships that is unhealthy fear. For those who get their identity in what they do, it is easy to understand how a marriage crisis or separation might push that person to work longer hours as an escape. This is an unhealthy fear that is founded on a lie that what we do is more important than people. Ask anyone, at the end of their life, if they wish they had worked longer hours instead of spending more time with their children or grandchildren. The answer is obvious.

Proactive Tips

- Budget your work schedule. As discussed in Lesson Two, financial obligations double when couples separate. Be careful not to put work above friends and family, especially if you have children. Unhealthy financial fear habits take place gradually and can begin even among couples who are not in crisis. Work can become a hiding place for not having to deal with people, problems, or life.

- Consider taking at least one day each week just to spend with family and friends. If you have children (regardless of their ages), it speaks volumes when you take time to have lunch or dinner or spend time doing what they enjoy.

- Ask for input. Friends and family are the ones who suffer when a person puts more energy into their work instead of their relationships, and if you ask if they feel that you work too much, they will let you know.

- Nothing is more important than keeping relationships intact, and fear of not having enough money is often the main reason for not doing so.

4. Unexplained Illnesses

As mentioned at the beginning of this lesson, the emotion of fear produces adrenalin for the purpose of fighting or fleeing in dangerous situations. If we remain in the fight-or-flight state indefinitely, the extra adrenalin wreaks havoc on our bodies. God designed our minds and bodies to be replenished when we sleep, and if we are in a constant state of fear, it is impossible to replenish. Health professionals agree that stress and lack of sleep are the cause for many unexplained illnesses. When a couple separates, it is not uncommon for one or both spouses to live with ongoing stress due to unresolved arguments and an unhealthy fear of what the future may hold. Be wise when it comes to your health, and practice the following tips.

Proactive Tips

- Physical exercise is the best way to release adrenalin from your body. Aerobic exercise is best, but any exercise is better than none. If joining a gym or class is too difficult, consider walking, bike riding, or swimming. By being physically active, you will also help your mental outlook, since exercise produces a chemical called norepinephrine that moderates our brain's response to stress.

- Get professional help if you need it. If you find that worry, and stress, and unhealthy fears are keeping you from getting out of bed and leading a normal productive life, see your healthcare professional, and get the help you need. Ongoing stress can lead to mental health issues such as depression, and you may need professional help to get you through. Referrals from faith-based organizations can be helpful. (Contact our organization for more information.)

- Be cautious and informed before taking prescription-drugs. Most stress due to unhealthy fears can be managed through exercise and counseling, but your health-care professional may prescribe medication as well. While there are prescription-drugs for nearly everything nowadays, all have side effects. So, before taking medications for stress, be well informed and under a doctor's care.

- Create a safe and comfortable sleeping environment. If being alone in the evenings causes you to feel anxious for any reason, make the necessary changes. Some men, whose wives have initiated the separation, have said that evenings are extremely stressful, because they feel that they should be protecting their wife or children from harm. In addition, we have heard from many women who felt afraid and unable to sleep once their husband was no longer in the home. Express your concerns to people you trust and who will help you come up with solutions.

Scripture Reading

Pray first, and read the following Scriptures. Read the surrounding verses, to help you with the context. Answer the questions on a separate piece of paper or in your journal, if you need more space.

Read Psalm 37: 1-6

- In verses 1 and 2, what are you to avoid worrying about and whom are you not supposed to envy?

- What does verse 3 tell us to do? What will be our reward?

- In verses 4-6, we are told to take delight in the Lord, and He will give us our heart's desires. What do you think should be our number one heart's desire based on verses 5 and 6?

- What does verse 7 say about God's timing?

- Based on verses 18-19, how should you respond when faced with situations that cause you to live with unhealthy fears?

- What do verses 39 and 40 promise?

For You to Consider

Do a search on your own for verses that deal with fear and worry. Choose at least five verses to memorize this year, and discuss these verses in your group or with your accountability partner.

EMOTIONAL INSTABLILITY

Let your conversation be gracious and attractive so that you will have the right response for everyone.

—

Colossians 4:6

If you have ever had a flat tire or skidded across black ice, you know what it is like to lose control while driving. With proper training, an experienced driver can usually maneuver their car to safety. The same is true for couples who lose control of their emotions when in crisis. When men and women have experience and proper training, emotions can be brought under control before too much damage is done. Couples in crisis are dealing with about 25% of their emotional capacity, and most law enforcement officials agree that domestic violence calls are the most dangerous to respond to.

While the word "control" often refers to negative behavior, this lesson is about positive behavior and learning to control your emotions in the midst of your crisis. You don't have to be a victim of your circumstances, and you can prevail, regardless of what happens in your marriage. Your relationship with God can grow, and you can mature emotionally and spiritually by learning to be proactive rather than reactive.

Common Times for Emotional Instability

1. Parenting Challenges

When a physical separation occurs, parenting is often more stressful. Even a parent who is easygoing, can fall into a bad habit of having outbursts or saying things in anger because of heightened emotions. Sadly, children are the ones to pay the price. If you are struggling in the area of parenting, being proactive will be important for your whole family. Positive parenting changes will not happen overnight, but your efforts will not go unnoticed, and your children will benefit. Regardless of how your spouse is behaving, you can be the one to set a good example for the sake of your children.

From Andy

My wife and I were separated for a couple of months. In the beginning, I wanted to spend time with my boys, but my wife's family had taken over and did not want us getting back together. This caused emotions to run high, which resulted in huge arguments with the whole family. Things have been said and done that can never be taken back. Even after we reconciled, we continued to deal with the consequences for over a year.

Proactive Tips

- Make a solid commitment never to speak badly about your spouse to your children or other family members. If you have spoken badly about your spouse, it is never too late to repent and apologize.

- If you have addictions, anger, or other issues that would cause your spouse to win a custody battle in court, take classes or get counseling. Courts want both parents involved in the raising of children, so do your best to have parental rights.

- Think of your children before you think of yourself. If you are exhibiting behavior that you would not want to teach your children, or if you are trying to pit your children against your spouse or other family members in any way, stop. Don't let your emotions get out of control.

- Ask a family member, or even your children, if there is anything you should change in order to be a better parent. (Some couples are on good enough terms to have this conversation, but be cautious since hot-button topics can cause emotions to escalate quickly.)

- Take a parenting class. Most are designed to provide communication skills that also strengthen adult relationships. We have known several couples who were separated and felt less intimidated by taking a parenting class rather than a marriage class. In many cases, the parenting class resulted in reconciliation.

- Pray for your spouse daily. Even if you think reconciliation is impossible, the supernatural power of prayer can help soften your heart as well as your responses. Be the parent that your children need.

2. **Your Spouse's Behavior**

If you are separated, the input you once had as to where your spouse went, how long they were gone, and even what they ate or chose to wear, is now gone. This can cause you to overact when your spouse behaves in ways that are embarrassing or frustrating. Regardless, you will have to learn to be proactive in this area, if you want any chance at all of reconciliation. Emotional outbursts will only confirm to an unwilling spouse that he or she is better off alone or with someone new.

Proactive Tips

- Consider joining a co-dependency support group that will help you learn new proactive responses when you are feeling frustrated with your spouse's behavior.

- Read books that address healthy boundary issues (faith-based is best).

- Pray for God to show you when you are trying to control anyone other than yourself.

- Ignore embarrassing behavior from your spouse. In a social-media-gone-mad world, actions from an emotionally immature spouse can be humiliating for the whole family. Unless your spouse is doing something illegal or dangerous, most behavior can be viewed as immature and is best left alone.

3. **Physical or Mental Health Reasons**

If you or your spouse suffer from a physical illness or have mental-health issues, it will be more difficult to respond to frustrations in an emotionally adult manner. Even if physical or mental illness is not an issue, some people are more prone to emotional meltdowns than others. As mentioned previously, stressful situations can affect our ability to get good sleep and eat properly, which play a huge role in mental and physical health. Sleep deprivation can mimic mental illness, which, of course, leaves a person unable to keep their emotional responses in check.

From Rick

My wife started exhibiting signs of mental illness after our 4th child was born. When our daughter was only a few months old, my wife left the home and was gone for several days before the authorities found her wandering in the streets. It took several months to get her the medication and help that she needed. For the past several years, we have had ups and downs due to medication side-effects and her decision to stop taking meds at times. This has been hard on the whole family, but my daughters (who are now in their 20's) have said many times that my ability to stay calm and loving in the midst of it all helped them to cope. Without the support of our church, the doctors, and my faith, I don't think I would have been much of an example to anyone.

Proactive Tips

- If you have been under a doctor's care for physical or mental illness prior to your separation, make an effort to keep your physician in the loop with your current situation. Do not begin or stop taking medications without informing your health-care professional.

- As mentioned in the previous lesson, exercise can provide the endorphins your body and mind need to stay healthy. These "feel-good brain chemicals" are released with regular exercise and can make a huge difference in your mood, and possibly even ease depression. (See Mayo Clinic website for more on the importance of exercise and mental health.)

- Read faith-based books on spiritual maturity and proactive living. Authors Henry Cloud and John Townsend have written several books on how having good boundaries, making wise choices, and living life as God intended affects our mental and physical health positively.

- Practice replacing negative thinking with a Bible verse. Our minds were created by God with the ability to meditate. We can meditate on negative things, which result in worry, or we can meditate on good things and allow God to replace fear, anxiety, and anger with His love.

Emotionally immature behavior nearly always results in negative consequences. Regardless of what happens in your marriage, learning to control your emotions is vital to living a better life, and one that will glorify God.

Scripture Reading

Pray first, then read the following Scriptures with surrounding verses, and answer the questions. Use a journal or separate piece of paper if you need more space.

1. Read 1 Peter 1:13-16

   - What does Peter say to do if you consider yourself a follower of Jesus Christ?

   - In verse 14, what does Peter warn against?

2. Read 1 Peter 3:8-12

   - In verses 8-9, what does Peter tell all Christians to do?

   - In verses 10-11, make a list of all the actions Peter lists from Scriptures.

   - According to verse 12, what is an even more important reason for doing the right thing?

For You to Consider

Based on this week's lesson, is there something you can start doing now in order to have better control of your emotions? Is there a behavior you need to change immediately? Is there someone you need to apologize to? Ask God for wisdom, and have people praying for you.

LOSS OF IDENTITY

I am the light of the world. If you follow me, you won't have to walk in darkness, because you will have the light that leads to life.

—

John 8:12

Since a person's marital status is an integral part of their identity, it is easy to understand why separation and divorce can be so devastating. When the spouse who leaves behaves as though he or she were single, it is even more difficult for the one who still identifies as being married.

If you are feeling a loss of identity because of your separation, don't lose hope. Along with turning to God and placing your trust in Him, the following tips will help you avoid feeling a loss of identity while your marital status is on hold.

Common Times to Feel a Loss of Identity

1. When Asked to Define Your Marital Status

It will not be easy avoiding questions that have to do with your marital status. Simply filling out an information form can be a reminder that even though you are still legally married, your spouse no longer lives at the same address. If you have children in school, filling out new parental consent or change of address forms can also be emotionally draining. You cannot avoid the questions, but you can be prepared with how to answer.

Proactive Tips

- As mentioned in earlier lessons, if you are separated, you are still married. While God created each of us individually, He supernaturally joins a man and woman when they marry, and they become as "one" (see Genesis 2:24). Unless your spouse dies or divorces you, it is best to think of yourself as married.

- When filling out an information form, which includes the option of "separated," consider marking "married" since you are, in fact, still legally married. (This may also help alleviate additional questions from people reading the information form.)

2. **Frequenting Places That You and Your Spouse Went to Together**

When a spouse dies, the spouse left behind has a new status of "widow" or "widower." The person must learn to adjust in the area of frequenting favorite places he or she once attended with their spouse or attending events alone. Even though your spouse is still alive, your adjustment can be much the same. Making a reservation or registering for an event, as an individual rather than as a couple, can be an unwelcomed reminder that you are no longer a "couple." Still, life is meant to be enjoyed, and it will be important not to give up the things that make you happy.

Proactive Tips

- The next time you plan to make reservations or purchase event tickets, consider purchasing two, with the plan of inviting a friend or relative to join you.

- If you plan to go somewhere that you and your spouse enjoyed as a couple, choose different seats and new foods or drinks off the menu when possible.

3. **When You are Feeling Sad**

It is true that breakups are painful, especially in marriage. If you are sad and feel a loss of identity due to your broken heart, it is important to remember that God is in control. He is not wringing His hands wondering what will happen next. He knew the day you would come into this world, and He knew whom you would marry. He also knew when your marriage would be in crisis. And, He knows the rest of your life's journey and when you will leave this world and go to Him for eternity. If you focus on Him, and trust Him when you are sad, He will replace the pain with joy. It is been said that God allows a broken heart so that He can enter into it easier. As mentioned in the beginning of this lesson, trust God, and turn to Him. He promises to work this all out for good, if you love Him and follow His ways (see Romans 8:28).

From Michelle

When Joe and I first separated, even though there was a sense of relief because all the arguing had subsided in the home, it was hard to look at photos. My heart ached when I saw times of happiness and remembered how much fun we had together when we weren't in crisis. I remember looking at photos of our wedding day and remembering our honeymoon. The pain in my heart was a reminder that I was separated. I think the loss of identity I felt was more about our whole family being separated—not just Joe and I. It was during the second year of our separation that I began to feel a new identity in Christ, and there began to be a joy in my heart again. I do believe that finding that inner peace and joy is what helped our marriage to be saved.

Proactive Tips

- Let yourself grieve. Sadness is to be expected when a marriage is in crisis. If you are separated, and your spouse is not willing to reconcile at this point, don't pretend that you are happy if you are sad. Give yourself time to grieve the loss.

- Get up, and do the next best thing. If you have a job, children, and obligations, you will not be able to live the rest of your life grieving. Every day, get up and do what needs to be done. Even when you are sad, you can still take care of your obligations and help others. (As mentioned in earlier lessons, get the help you need if you are unable to manage your emotions.)

- Even if you are sad, don't avoid looking at photos of happier times. As Michelle explained, even though looking at photos was sometimes painful, it was also a reminder that there was a hole in her heart that needed to be filled. Her broken heart made it easier to turn her life to Christ. (If photos do the opposite, and instead cause you to remember times that were not happy, then of course put them away, and trust God to do His work in you and your spouse's heart without photos.)

4. Shared Parenting

To go from full-time parent to part-time parent is difficult for most moms and dads. We rarely see a separation or divorce where the children are not affected. The identity of everyone in the family changes the moment a separation takes place.

From Steve

Before my wife left, I was a full-time husband, and a dad to our son and daughter. After she moved out, I became a part-time dad and not a husband to her at all. When her boyfriend moved in, it got worse. My children even referred to him as their "daddy" at times. We were separated for nearly a year before she filed for a divorce and married her boyfriend. It has been a couple of years, and I have finally gotten used to being a part-time dad, but it still hurts. I did not realize that I would struggle so much with having my kids not live with me all of the time. I have heard people say that men get their identity in what they do, while women get their identity from relationships. In my case, I have to say that my identity was in being a husband and a dad over what I did in my job. I don't like the terms "Disneyland Dad" or "Weekend Dad," but I guess that's what society has labeled and identified divorced dads, who have part-time custody of their children.

Proactive Tips

- Keep your emotions in check. Guard against becoming bitter or having an emotional meltdown in front of your children when you feel lost as to what your role or input in their life may be. You are still their mom or dad, regardless of having to share custody.

- Realize that when your children go to your spouse's home, they may feel disloyal by showing affection or having a good time, particularly if there is third party involvement. The best gift you can give your child is to take the pressure off. When they leave your house, hug them and tell them to have a good time. When they return to your home, smile, and ask how their time was. Regardless of what they say or how they word it, listen and be there for them. If their time did not go well have empathy, but keep your emotions in check. If they had fun, be happy with them. Be a mature parent, regardless of how your spouse behaves.

- Provide a safe place for your children to be authentic. Showing unconditional love to your children will help them to share their true feelings as they learn to adjust to their family's new identity. This does not mean you will not have boundaries, rules, and guidelines, but implement them with a soft heart.

- Avoid excessively spoiling your children in an attempt to make up for what your spouse is not providing or, even worse, to win their affections from the other parent.

- Your identity as a parent is as important as it is in your marital status. Your role as mom or dad will be there as long as your children are alive on this earth—regardless of their age. They will suffer enough in this world, but don't let the suffering come from you. In the long run, you will be better off for it, and so will they.

Keep your focus on God, and remember that your self-worth and identity come from Him.

God created you as an individual, with a unique personality, gifts, and DNA that no one else on earth has. He also created you with the ability to persevere through the storms in life. Jesus said, "Here on earth you will have many trials and sorrows. But take heart, because I have overcome the world" (John 16:33). God wants your identity to be in Him, in order to trust Him in times of trouble. If you have put your faith in Him, He is by your side now and will never leave you.

Scripture Reading

Pray first, then read the following Scriptures with surrounding verses, and answer the questions. Use a journal or separate piece of paper, if you need more space.

1. Read Matthew 22:29-30. What does Jesus say about marriage after death?

2. Read Matthew 22:37-40. What does Jesus say are the two most important commandments?

3. Read John 12:35-36. What does Jesus want you to do, and how does He refer to us?

4. Read Colossians 2:6-10. What does Paul say you need to do once you make a commitment to follow Christ?

For You to Consider

Discuss with your group or accountability partner any of the tips in these lessons that you have implemented. Discuss which tools have been most effective. If you have not gone through the *Marriage 911: First Response* workbook, or Riding *the Waves of Tribulation in Your Marriage, God's Way* workbook, please visit our website for more information.

CONCLUDING REMARKS

From Joe and Michelle

Our children thank us often for making our marriage work and modeling a good marriage for their children. When couples reconcile, they often fall back into old behaviors. We reconciled a couple of times before we realized that just because we missed each other and moved back in together, it did not mean we could shift our focus from Christ to our spouse and the world again. Over the years, we have learned that keeping our eyes on God allows us to meet each other at the foot of the cross. Is it easy all of the time? Of course not. Is it worth it? Absolutely.

We know that some of you will reconcile and will possibly have an even better marriage than before you separated. That's what happens in many cases. Our advice is to never give up, no matter how impossible things look. Stay focused on growing in your relationship with God and be the best parent you can be if you have children.

Regardless of what your spouse chooses to do, we pray that you will use the tools in this workbook to stay on the line of reconciliation and wait, God's way. We hear from people all over the world who regret not waiting. We also hear from people who are thankful they waited. Waiting for a spouse to return or repent is not easy, but it can be a wonderful time to experience God's love without the distractions of marriage or needs of your spouse. If you will take this time to grow in your relationship and mature emotionally and spiritually, whatever the outcome is, it will be worth it.

There are many people who have come through this ministry whose lives are better simply because they turned from their old behaviors and followed Christ. Many have reconciled with their spouse. Some ended in an unwanted divorce. Some remarried in the Lord and now serve Him as a result of their pain and experience.

And some are still waiting—God's Way.

GROUP DISCUSSION AND FACILITATOR GUIDELINES

These guidelines are based on many years of conducting classes and small groups for couples and individuals whose marriages are in crisis. They aren't meant to constrain you in any way, but to help you avoid some of the mistakes leaders have experienced in the past. Feel free to adjust these guidelines accordingly, and contact our organization with any suggestions or questions.

Suggested Facilitator Qualifications

- The facilitator should be a married or single person who has a good relationship with people, and with God. The person should not be in the midst of a separation, or have a marriage in crisis.

- The facilitator needs to be the same gender as the group he or she is leading.

Recommended Group Setting

- Since this workbook is for people who are separated, we recommend that the discussion group not be co-ed. This helps protect someone in crisis, and vulnerable, from getting emotionally or intimately involved with someone of the opposite sex.

- The group can be held in a home or a public community setting.

- It is always best to focus the discussion time on the verses and questions provided in the lessons. This will help alleviate negative sharing or having the group end later than expected.

- After the group has completed the nine-week course, help each participant choose follow-up resources. Direct them to our website, or provide a list of available classes or groups in your church or community.

- Additional facilitator guidelines are available on our website.

Thank you for joining us in the ministry of reconciling marriages and families—God's Way

The International Center for Reconciling God's Way

www.icrgw.org

www.Marriage911Godsway.com

www.ingramcontent.com/pod-product-compliance
Lightning Source LLC
Chambersburg PA
CBHW080427030426
42335CB00020B/2622